AF798882

Maximizing Social Security Benefits

When to take it, how much you'll get and how to file with confidence

By Jeff Weidner

Boom Retirement Solutions

Copyright Notice:

Copyright © 2025 Boom Retirement Solutions. All Rights Reserved.

Published by Bom Retirement Solutions
Wake Forest, NC

No part of this publication may be reproduced, stored in a retrieval system, or transmitted in any form or by any means—electronic, mechanical, photocopying, recording, scanning, or otherwise—except as permitted under Sections 107 and 108 of the 1976 United States Copyright Act, without prior written permission of the publisher. Requests for permission should be directed to jeff@boomretirement.com.

Limited Liability and Disclaimer of Warranty:

Every effort has been made by the author and publisher to ensure the accuracy and completeness of this book. However, the publisher and author make no representations or warranties of any kind, express or implied, about the accuracy or completeness of the contents. They specifically disclaim all implied warranties of merchantability or fitness for a particular purpose.

The strategies and advice in this book may not be suitable for every situation. Neither the author nor the publisher shall be held liable for any loss of profit or other damages, including but not limited to special, incidental, consequential, or other damages arising out of the use or misuse of the information provided. Readers should consult with a qualified professional for personalized guidance.

First Edition
Published in Wake Forest, NC by Boom Retirement Solutions, 2025

Summary:

Every retiree should know how to maximize Social Security benefits, reduce tax liabilities, minimize Required Minimum Distributions (RMDs), and achieve financial success in retirement.

Author: Jeff Weidner

Dedication

To all those approaching retirement, may you find the confidence and clarity to make the most of social security, your retirement assets, reduce your taxes and create the retirement you deserve.

And to my family, whose support made this book possible.

Download your Free Book

https://books.jeffweidner.com/free

SCAN ME

DOWNLOAD FREE BOOK

Acknowledgments

Writing a book about Social Security that is both comprehensive and accessible requires the support and expertise of many individuals. I would like to express my deepest gratitude to:

My clients, whose questions and concerns helped shape the content of this book. Your trust in me to guide you through retirement planning decisions has been both a privilege and an inspiration.

The team at Boom Retirement Solutions, whose dedication to serving our clients with excellence provides the foundation for everything we do. Your commitment to helping people create secure retirement income strategies makes our work meaningful and impactful.

My mentors in the financial services industry, who taught me the importance of putting clients first and always continuing to learn. Your guidance has been invaluable in developing the expertise shared in these pages.

The editorial team, whose careful attention to detail helped ensure this complex subject matter is presented clearly and accurately. Your contributions have made this book more accessible and useful for readers.

My family, whose patience and support during the writing process made this book possible. Your encouragement kept me going through long hours of research and writing.

Finally, to you, the reader, for taking this important step toward understanding and maximizing your Social Security benefits. Your commitment to creating a secure retirement future is admirable.

How to Use This Book

This book is designed to help you understand and maximize your Social Security benefits. Each chapter builds upon the previous one, providing a comprehensive understanding of the Social Security system and how it fits into your retirement planning.

Key Features:

Real-World Examples: Throughout the book, you'll find stories of real people facing common Social Security decisions. These examples illustrate how different strategies can be applied to various situations.

Charts and Tables: Visual aids help clarify complex concepts and provide quick reference for important information.

Action Steps: Each chapter ends with specific steps you can take to apply what you've learned to your own situation.

Worksheets: The appendices contain practical worksheets to help you calculate your benefits, analyze your options, and create your retirement income plan.

Resource Directory: A comprehensive listing of additional resources and contact information is provided to help you access the support you need.

Table of Contents

Introduction:

Maximizing Social Security Benefits: When to Take It, How Much You'll Get, and How to File with Confidence

Picture this: You've worked hard your entire life, paying into Social Security with every paycheck, and now retirement is on the horizon. Like millions of Americans, you're probably wondering: "When should I start taking my benefits?" "How much will I actually receive?" and most importantly, "Will it be enough?"

You're not alone in asking these questions. Social Security represents one of the most important financial decisions you'll make in retirement, yet many Americans leave thousands of dollars on the table simply because they don't fully understand how the system works. This book aims to change that.

Why This Book Matters

Social Security isn't just another government program—it's the foundation of retirement security for most Americans. Consider these facts:

- For about half of seniors, Social Security provides at least 50% of their income
- For about 1 in 4 seniors, it provides 90% or more of their income
- Nearly 70 million Americans receive Social Security benefits

Despite its importance, many people make their claiming decisions without fully understanding their options. A rushed or uninformed choice about when to take Social Security can cost you tens of thousands of dollars over your retirement years.

Common Misconceptions

Over the years, I've heard many misconceptions about Social Security:

- "I need to claim as soon as possible because Social Security might run out"
- "Once I start taking benefits, I can't change my mind"
- "I can't work after I start receiving benefits"
- "Social Security alone will be enough for my retirement"

This book will help you separate fact from fiction and make informed decisions based on your unique situation.

What You'll Learn

In the following chapters, we'll cover:

- The basics of how Social Security works and who qualifies
- Strategic timing decisions that can maximize your benefits
- How to calculate your expected benefits and retirement income gap
- Step-by-step guidance on the filing process
- Advanced strategies for married couples
- Ways to coordinate Social Security with your other retirement income sources

We'll explore these topics using real-world examples, clear explanations, and practical worksheets. You'll find charts and graphs that break down complex concepts into easily digestible pieces, and each chapter ends with key takeaways to help reinforce important points.

A Note About Your Retirement Income

While Social Security provides a foundation for retirement, it was never designed to be your only source of retirement income. Throughout this book, we'll discuss how to identify and fill any gaps between your guaranteed income sources (like Social Security and pensions) and your monthly expenses. We'll explore how tools like Fixed Indexed Annuities with Guaranteed Income for Life riders can help provide the additional secure income you might need.

Your Next Steps

As you read through this book, keep your own situation in mind. Take notes, use the worksheets, and don't hesitate to revisit sections that are particularly relevant to your circumstances. Remember, the goal isn't just to understand Social Security—it's to help you make informed decisions that will enhance your retirement security.

Let's begin your journey toward maximizing your Social Security benefits and creating a more secure retirement future.

In the next chapter, we'll start with the fundamentals of Social Security, including its history, how it's funded, and who qualifies for benefits. This foundation will help you better understand the strategic decisions we'll discuss later in the book.

NOTE:

Social Security is a cornerstone of retirement planning for millions of Americans, providing a reliable income stream that often forms the foundation of their financial security. However, navigating the complexities of Social Security requires careful planning and a thorough understanding of how benefits are calculated, taxed, and integrated with other retirement strategies. This guide aims to empower you with actionable strategies to maximize your benefits, avoid common pitfalls, and make informed decisions about when and how to claim. By aligning Social Security with your broader retirement goals, you can achieve greater financial confidence and stability in your golden years.

Chapter 1: Understanding Social Security Basics

[illegible]

What Is Social Security?

[illegible]

How Social Security Is Funded

[illegible]

Chapter 1: Understanding Social Security Basics

When Jane Thompson turned 62, she was eager to start collecting Social Security benefits. "I've paid into the system for 40 years," she told me. "I want to make sure I get my money's worth." Like many Americans, Jane didn't realize that waiting a few years could significantly increase her monthly benefits. By understanding the basics of Social Security, she was able to make a more informed decision about when to claim.

What Is Social Security?

Social Security is more than just a retirement program—it's America's most successful anti-poverty program and a fundamental part of most people's retirement planning. Created in 1935 during the Great Depression, Social Security provides a safety net for retirees, disabled workers, and their families.

How Social Security Is Funded

Think of Social Security like a pay-as-you-go system. Today's workers pay taxes that fund current retirees' benefits. Here's a simple breakdown:

- Workers pay 6.2% of their earnings (up to a limit)
- Employers match this 6.2%
- Self-employed individuals pay both portions (12.4%)

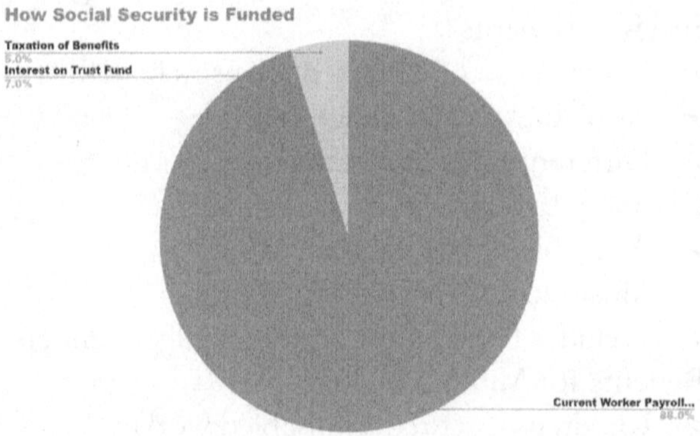

Who Qualifies for Benefits

To qualify for retirement benefits, you need to earn 40 "credits" throughout your working life. In 2025, you earn one credit for every $1,690 in covered earnings, up to four credits per year. Most people earn their 40 credits in 10 years of work.

Types of Social Security Benefits

Many Americans don't realize that Social Security offers more than just retirement benefits. Here are the main types:

- Retirement Benefits
  - Based on your work history and earnings
  - Available as early as age 62
  - Full benefits at your Full Retirement Age (FRA)
- Spousal Benefits
  - Up to 50% of your spouse's benefit

- Available even if you never worked
- Can switch to your own benefit if it's higher
- Survivor Benefits
  - Up to 100% of deceased spouse's benefit
  - Available as early as age 60
  - Different rules for disabled survivors
- Disability Benefits
  - Available before retirement age
  - Must meet specific medical criteria
  - Includes benefits for eligible family members
- Benefits for Minor Children
  - Children of retired or disabled workers
  - Must be under 18 (or 19 if still in high school)
  - Disabled children may receive lifetime benefits

Real-World Example: The Martinez Family

Consider the Martinez family. Robert worked as a teacher for 30 years before becoming disabled at age 58. Thanks to Social Security's comprehensive coverage:

- Robert receives disability benefits
- His wife Maria receives spousal benefits
- Their 16-year-old daughter receives benefits until she graduates
- If Robert passes away, his family will be eligible for survivor benefits

How Benefits Are Calculated

Your Social Security benefit is based on your highest 35 years of earnings, adjusted for inflation. Let's break this down into simple steps:

1. Your earnings are indexed for inflation

2. Your highest 35 years are selected

3. These earnings are averaged to create your AIME (Average Indexed Monthly Earnings)
4. A formula is applied to determine your Primary Insurance Amount (PIA)

Sample Earnings Impact on Benefits

	Retirement at Age 62			Retirement at Age 65		
		Monthly benefits			Monthly benefits	
Retirement in January	AIME	Initial	In 2025	AIME	Initial	In 2025
2024	13,100	2,710	2,778	11,256	3,426	3,512
2025	13,689	2,831	2,831	11,621	3,374	3,374

	Retirement at Age 66			Retirement at Age 67		
		Monthly benefits			Monthly benefits	
Retirement in January	AIME	Initial	In 2025	AIME	Initial	In 2025
2024	10,911	3,652	3,744	10,600	3,911	4,008
2025	11,351	3,795	3,795	11,017	4,043	4,043

	Retirement at Age 70		
		Monthly benefits	
Retirement in January	AIME	Initial	In 2025
2024	9,990	4,873	4,995
2025	10,367	5,108	5,108

Note: Figures are approximate and for illustration only, courtesy Social Security Administration website https://www.ssa.gov/oact/cola/examplemax.html

Full Retirement Age (FRA)

Retirement at age 62 is assumed here to be at exact age 62 and 1 month. Such early retirement results in a reduced monthly benefit.

Retirement at age 65 is assumed to be at exact age 65 and 0 months. For retirement in 2003 and later, the monthly benefit is reduced for early retirement. (For people born before 1938, age 65 is the normal retirement age. Normal retirement age will gradually increase to age 67.)

Retirement at age 66 is assumed to be at exact age 66 and 0 months. Age 66 is the normal retirement age for people born in 1943-54. People who retired at age 66 and who were born before 1943 received delayed retirement credits; those born after 1954 will have their benefits reduced for early retirement. Thus, for retirement in 2021 and later, the monthly benefit is reduced for early retirement.

Retirement at age 67 is assumed to be at exact age 67 and 0 months. Age 67 is the normal retirement age for people born in 1960 and later. People who retired at age 67 and who were born before 1960 received delayed retirement credits.
Retirement at age 70 maximizes the effect of delayed retirement credits.

Common Calculation Mistakes to Avoid

- Assuming all years count equally
- Forgetting about the earnings cap
- Not checking your earnings record
- Misunderstanding how working affects benefits

Interacting with the Social Security Administration (SSA)

The SSA offers several ways to access their services:

- Online through www.ssa.gov (available 24/7)
- By phone at 1-800-772-1213
- In person at local offices (by appointment)

Getting Help

Create a 'my Social Security' account online to:

- Review your earnings history
- Get benefit estimates
- Download benefit verification letters
- Change your address or direct deposit information

Chapter Summary

✓ Social Security provides multiple types of benefits ✓ You need 40 credits to qualify for retirement benefits ✓ Benefits are based on your highest 35 years of earnings ✓ The SSA offers various ways to access services ✓ Creating an online account gives you easy access to important information

Action Steps

1. Create your my Social Security account

2. Review your earnings history for accuracy

3. Get an estimate of your future benefits

4. List all family members who might be eligible for benefits

5. Write down any questions to discuss with a financial professional

In the next chapter, we'll explore one of the most important decisions you'll make: when to take your Social Security benefits. You'll learn how timing affects your payment amounts and strategies for choosing the best time to claim.

NOTE:

Social Security benefits are calculated based on your 35 highest-earning years and adjusted for inflation. To maximize benefits, consider your full retirement age (FRA), which varies based on your birth year, and the impact of claiming early or delaying benefits. Claiming before FRA reduces benefits permanently, while delaying increases them up to age 70. Additionally, Social Security benefits may be subject to federal income tax if your combined income exceeds certain thresholds. Consult a financial advisor to develop a strategy that aligns Social Security with your overall retirement plan.

Chapter 2: When to Take Social Security

Bob and Mary Johnson sat across from me, wrestling with a decision that millions of Americans face each year. "We're both turning 62 soon," Bob explained. "Should we take Social Security now or wait?" This common question doesn't have a one-size-fits-all answer, but understanding the impact of timing can help you make the best choice for your situation.

The Importance of Timing

Your monthly Social Security benefit amount can vary by as much as 77% depending on when you start taking it. Let's explore why timing matters so much.

Age Options for Taking Benefits

You have three main options:

1. **Early Claiming (62-66):** Results in lower lifetime monthly benefits but may suit those needing immediate income, retire earlier or with shorter life expectancy.

2. **Claiming at FRA (66-67):** Provides the full benefit amount without reductions or bonuses.

3. **Delayed Claiming (67-70):** Maximizes monthly benefits, ideal for those that plan to work longer, with longer life expectancy, or other sources of retirement income.

Note: Based on Full Retirement Age of 67

Percentage Impact of Different Claiming Ages

- Age 62: Receive 70% of your full benefit
- Full Retirement Age: Receive 100% of your benefit
- Age 70: Receive 132% of your full benefit

Understanding Full Retirement Age (FRA)

Your Full Retirement Age depends on when you were born:

Full Retirement Age	
Birth Year	Full Retirement Age
1943-1954	66 years old
1955	66 and two months
1956	66 and four months
1957	66 and six months
1958	66 and eight months
1959	66 and 10 months
1960 and later	67 years old

Factors to Consider When Choosing When to Claim

1. Life Expectancy

- Family health history
- Personal health status
- Lifestyle factors
- Gender (women typically live longer)

2. Financial Needs

- Current income sources

- Expected expenses
- Debt obligations
- Emergency savings

3. Employment Status

- Planning to work?
- Earnings limits
- Tax implications

4. Marital Status

- Spouse's age and benefits
- Coordination strategies
- Survivor benefit considerations

Break-Even Analysis

Understanding your break-even point can help with timing decisions. Here's a real-world example:

Sarah has a full retirement benefit of $2,000 per month at age 67. Let's compare her cumulative benefits under different scenarios:

Early Claiming (Age 62):

- Monthly benefit: $1,400
- By age 80: $302,400 total

Full Retirement Age (67):

- Monthly benefit: $2,000
- By age 80: $312,000 total

Delayed Claiming (Age 70):

- Monthly benefit: $2,480
- By age 80: $297,600 total

In this case, Sarah's break-even point between claiming at 62 versus 67 is age 78. If she expects to live beyond 78, waiting until 67 would provide more lifetime benefits.

Case Studies: Timing Strategies

Case Study 1: Claiming Early for Financial Necessity

Tom lost his job at 62 and needed income. Despite the reduced benefit, claiming early made sense because:

- He had immediate income needs
- His health was declining
- He had other savings to supplement income
- His spouse had her own substantial benefit

Case Study 2: Delaying for Higher Payouts

Linda chose to wait until 70 because:

- She was still working
- She had good health and family longevity
- She wanted maximum survivor benefits for her younger spouse
- She had adequate savings to bridge the gap

Working While Receiving Benefits

If you claim benefits before your FRA and continue working, be aware of the earnings limit:

- In 2025, you can earn up to $22,320 without penalty
- Benefits are reduced by $1 for every $2 earned above this limit
- The limit increases the year you reach FRA
- After FRA, there is no earnings limit

Making Your Decision

Consider these key questions:

1. Can you afford to wait for higher benefits?
2. How is your health and family longevity?
3. Are you still working?
4. How will your decision affect your spouse?
5. What other retirement income sources do you have?

Creating Your Social Security Timing Strategy

Use this simple worksheet to evaluate your situation:

1. List your estimated monthly benefits at:
   - Age 62: $_______
   - Your FRA: $_______
   - Age 70: $_______
2. Calculate your expected monthly expenses: $_______
3. Identify other income sources:
   - Pension: $_______

- o 401(k)/IRA distributions: $_______
- o Other: $_______

4. Calculate your potential income gap: $_______

Chapter Summary

✓ The timing of your Social Security claim significantly impacts your benefit amount ✓ Your Full Retirement Age depends on your birth year ✓ Consider health, finances, employment, and marital status when deciding ✓ Working while receiving early benefits may reduce your payments ✓ Understanding break-even points can help inform your decision

Action Steps

1. Determine your Full Retirement Age
2. Calculate your benefits at different ages
3. Evaluate your health and family longevity
4. Review your current and expected expenses
5. Consider seeking professional guidance for your specific situation

In the next chapter, we'll explore exactly how much you can expect to receive from Social Security and how to maximize your benefits through various strategies.

NOTE:

Deciding when to take Social Security depends on factors like your health, life expectancy, marital status, income needs, and whether you plan to continue working. Claiming benefits before your full retirement age (FRA) reduces your monthly payments permanently; while delaying them past FRA increases payments by up to 8% annually until age 70. Consider how spousal benefits, survivor benefits, and potential taxation of benefits impact your decision. A personalized strategy can help optimize your benefits and meet your long-term retirement goals.

Chapter 3: How Much Will You Get?

Margaret, a 58-year-old nurse with three decades of experience, sat in my office holding her latest Social Security statement. "I've been getting these statements for years," she said, "but I honestly don't understand what all these numbers mean." Like Margaret, many Americans find their Social Security statements confusing and struggle to understand exactly how much they'll receive in retirement. Let's demystify these numbers and help you understand precisely what you can expect.

Reading Your Social Security Statement

Your Social Security statement is more than just a piece of paper – it's a snapshot of your financial future. When you receive your statement, you'll notice several different benefit amounts listed. These aren't random numbers; they represent different scenarios based on when you choose to claim your benefits.

The statement shows your estimated monthly benefit at three crucial ages: early retirement at 62, full retirement age (typically 66-67), and delayed retirement at 70. Each of these numbers tells an important story about your potential retirement income. Let's look at a typical example to understand what these numbers mean in real life.

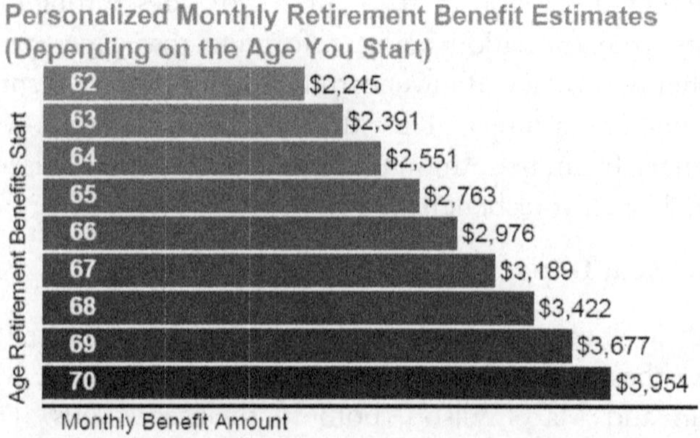

Go to http://SSA.gov to get your personalized benefit payout amounts

How Social Security Calculates Your Benefits

The process of calculating your Social Security benefit is like assembling a financial puzzle. The Social Security Administration looks at your entire working career, focusing on your highest-earning 35 years. This is why those final working years can be so important – they often replace lower-earning early career years in the calculation.

Think of it this way: imagine your earnings history as a bucket of 35 marbles, each representing a year of work. The Social Security Administration takes these marbles, adjusts them for inflation (called indexing), and then averages them together. This creates what's called your Average Indexed Monthly Earnings, or AIME.

But they don't stop there. Your AIME goes through one more transformation using a formula that gives you a higher percentage of lower earnings and a lower percentage of higher earnings. This final number becomes your Primary Insurance Amount (PIA) – the base figure used to calculate all your benefits.

The Real Impact on Real People

Let's look at a typical American household to understand how these calculations play out in the real world. Meet John and Mary Wilson, both in their early 60s. Their combined household income is $75,000, and they're trying to plan for retirement. Like many Americans, they're wondering if Social Security will be enough.

The Wilsons have typical monthly expenses of $4,000. When they add up their expected Social Security benefits ($2,800 combined) and John's small pension ($500), they discover they'll have a monthly income gap of $700. This gap between guaranteed income and expenses is a common challenge for retirees, but understanding it is the first step toward solving it.

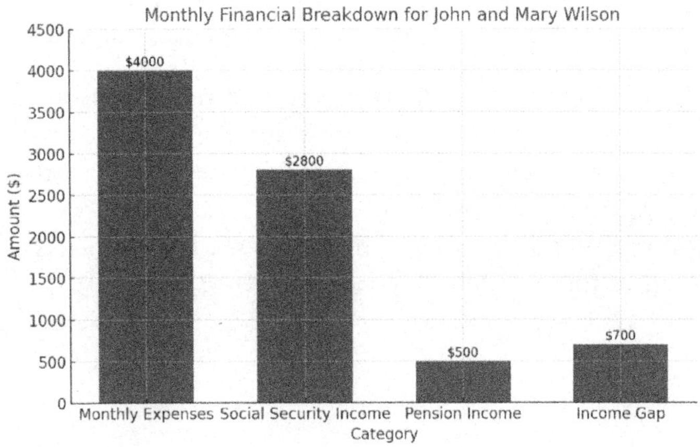

Understanding Cost of Living Adjustments

Your Social Security benefit isn't frozen in time. Each year, the Social Security Administration evaluates whether to increase benefits based on changes in the cost of living. These Cost of Living Adjustments (COLAs) help protect your purchasing power against inflation.

Think of COLAs like an annual raise for retirees. While the exact amount varies year to year based on inflation, recent history shows average increases of 2-3% annually. Over time, these increases can significantly impact your total benefits. For example, a $2,000 monthly benefit today could grow to $2,600 or more in ten years, assuming average COLAs.

The Impact of Working While Receiving Benefits

Many retirees are surprised to learn they can continue working while receiving Social Security benefits. However, if you claim benefits before reaching your full retirement age, there are some important rules to understand about how working affects your payments.

The Social Security Administration implements an earnings test for early retirees. Think of it like a seesaw – as your earnings go up, your benefits might temporarily go down. However, these reductions aren't permanent. Once you reach full retirement age, your benefits are recalculated to credit you for any months where benefits were withheld due to working.

The Tax Reality of Social Security Benefits

Understanding how Social Security benefits are taxed is crucial for effective retirement planning. Your benefits may be taxable if your combined income (adjusted gross income + nontaxable interest + half of your Social Security benefits) exceeds certain thresholds. This doesn't mean all your benefits are taxed – the amount subject to tax depends on your total income and filing status.

For example, a married couple filing jointly might pay no taxes on their Social Security if their combined income is under $32,000. However, up to 50% of their benefits could be taxable if their income falls between $32,000 and $44,000, and up to 85% could be taxable above $44,000.

Creating Your Retirement Income Plan

Understanding how much you'll receive from Social Security is just the first step. The key is developing a comprehensive plan that addresses any gaps between your guaranteed income and expenses. Let's walk through the process of creating this plan.

First, take a careful look at your monthly expenses. Include everything from essential costs like housing, healthcare, and food to discretionary spending like entertainment and travel. Be realistic – most people's expenses don't dramatically decrease in retirement.

Next, add up your guaranteed income sources. This includes Social Security benefits, any pension payments, and existing annuity income. The difference between your expenses and guaranteed income is your income gap – the amount you'll need to fund from other sources.

For many retirees, a Fixed Indexed Annuity with a Guaranteed Income for Life rider provides an excellent solution for filling this gap. These products offer several advantages: they provide guaranteed lifetime income, protect your principal from market downturns, and can include options for inflation protection and spousal continuation.

Planning for Your Future

As you review your Social Security statement and consider your retirement income needs, remember that Social Security was never designed to be your only source of retirement income. While it provides an important foundation, most retirees need additional sources of guaranteed income to maintain their desired lifestyle.

Consider working with a financial professional who can help you understand your Social Security benefits in the context of your overall retirement plan. They can help you identify potential income gaps and suggest appropriate solutions, such as Fixed Indexed Annuities, to ensure you have enough guaranteed income to cover your essential expenses.

Chapter Summary

Understanding your Social Security benefits requires looking at several key factors: your earnings history, claiming age, cost of living adjustments, and tax implications. By taking the time to understand these elements and how they affect your benefits, you can make more informed decisions about your retirement income strategy.

In the next chapter, we'll walk through the step-by-step process of actually filing for Social Security benefits, including how to avoid common mistakes and handle special situations that might arise during the application process.

NOTE:

Your Social Security benefit amount is based on your average indexed monthly earnings (AIME) during your 35 highest-earning years. The Social Security Administration (SSA) applies a formula to calculate your primary insurance amount (PIA), which determines your monthly benefit at full retirement age (FRA). Keep in mind that working fewer than 35 years will result in zero-earning years being factored into your calculation, reducing your benefit. Additionally, benefits are adjusted annually for cost-of-living increases (COLA) to keep pace with inflation. To estimate your benefit, use the SSA\u2019s online calculators or review your annual Social Security statement. For a more accurate projection, factor in the impact of claiming early, delaying benefits, or working beyond FRA.

Chapter 4: How to File for Social Security

[illegible]

Beginning Your Social Security Journey

[illegible]

Chapter 4: How to File for Social Security

Susan sat in my office, a thick folder of papers spread across my desk. Her hands nervously shuffled through Social Security statements, tax returns, and various identification documents. "There are so many forms and requirements," she said, her voice tinged with anxiety. "I'm afraid I'll make a mistake that will cost me money or delay my benefits." This is a concern I hear often, but with the right guidance, filing for Social Security can be straightforward and stress-free.

Beginning Your Social Security Journey

The key to a smooth filing process lies in careful preparation. Think of applying for Social Security as embarking on an important journey – one that requires proper planning and the right documentation. Three months before you want your benefits to begin, start gathering your essential documents. You'll need your Social Security card and birth certificate to prove your identity. For those who are married, divorced, or widowed, marriage certificates and divorce decrees tell the story of your family status. Recently retired? Your most recent W-2 forms or tax returns help verify your latest earnings.

A monthly timeline showing key preparation steps and milestones from initial planning through first payment

The Digital Gateway: Your Online Account

The Social Security Administration has embraced the digital age, making online access a cornerstone of their service delivery. Creating your my Social Security account serves as your digital key to the system. This account isn't just for filing – it's a powerful tool you'll use throughout your retirement years to manage your benefits.

Setting up your account requires careful attention to security. The Social Security Administration will verify your identity through a series of questions about your financial history. While this might seem cumbersome, think of it as the digital equivalent of showing your ID at a bank. The extra security steps protect your benefits from fraud and ensure that only you have access to your information.

Three Paths to Filing

The Social Security Administration offers three distinct ways to file for benefits, each with its own advantages. The online application has become the most popular option, offering convenience and flexibility. Imagine sitting at your kitchen table, coffee in hand, filing for benefits at your own pace. The process typically takes about 30 minutes, but you can save your progress and return later if needed.

For those who prefer a more personal touch, filing by phone provides a middle ground between digital convenience and human interaction. When you call the Social Security Administration, a representative will schedule a phone appointment. During this call, they'll guide you through the same questions you'd find online, but with the ability to ask questions and receive immediate clarification.

In-person applications at your local Social Security office remain valuable, particularly for those with complex situations. However, the days of walking in without an appointment are largely gone. You'll need to schedule your visit in advance, but this preparation ensures you'll have dedicated time with a representative who can address your specific needs.

Understanding What Happens After You Apply

Once you submit your application, a carefully orchestrated process begins. The Social Security Administration first reviews your application for completeness. They verify your identity, work history, and eligibility for benefits. This initial review typically takes a few weeks.

During this time, you might receive requests for additional documentation. Respond to these promptly – missing or delayed documents can extend the processing time. The Administration will also review your earnings record, ensuring all your work history is properly credited to your account.

Most applications receive a decision within 30 to 60 days. If approved, you'll receive an award letter detailing your benefit amount and when payments will begin. Remember that Social Security pays benefits the month after they're due. For example, your July benefit arrives in August.

Essential Documentation Checklist

While specific needs vary by situation, these core documents form the foundation of most applications:

- Birth certificate or other proof of age
- Social Security card or record of your number
- Recent W-2 forms or self-employment tax returns
- Marriage certificate (if applicable)
- Military discharge papers (if applicable)
- Bank account information for direct deposit

Navigating Special Circumstances

Some life situations require additional attention during the filing process. For divorced individuals seeking benefits on an ex-spouse's record, the process requires careful documentation of the marriage's duration and current marital status. However, you don't need to contact your ex-spouse or obtain their permission – the Social Security Administration handles this discreetly.

International retirees face unique challenges. If you plan to live abroad, understanding how Social Security handles international payments becomes crucial. Some countries have agreements with the United States that affect benefit payments, while others may have restrictions. The Social Security Administration can provide specific guidance based on your destination country.

When Things Don't Go As Planned

Despite careful preparation, sometimes applications face challenges. If your application is denied, don't lose hope. The appeals process provides multiple opportunities to present your case. The first step, called reconsideration, must be requested within 60 days of receiving your denial notice. A different reviewer will examine your application and any new evidence you provide.

If reconsideration doesn't succeed, you can request a hearing before an Administrative Law Judge. While this sounds formal, these hearings are designed to be accessible and fair. You can bring representation, present evidence, and explain your situation directly to the judge.

Coordinating With Medicare

For many retirees, Social Security filing coincides with Medicare enrollment. The timing here is critical. Medicare's Initial Enrollment Period begins three months before you turn 65 and continues for three months after. Missing this window can result in permanent penalties, so marking these dates on your calendar is essential.

If you're already receiving Social Security benefits when you turn 65, Medicare enrollment happens automatically for Parts A and B. However, you'll need to actively enroll in Part D (prescription drug coverage) if you want it. These decisions deserve careful consideration as they affect both your healthcare coverage and your budget.

Managing Income During the Transition

The weeks between filing and receiving your first benefit payment require careful financial planning. Many retirees find that a Fixed Indexed Annuity with a Guaranteed Income for Life rider provides valuable stability during this transition period. These products offer reliable monthly income while protecting your principal from market volatility.

Looking Ahead

Once your benefits begin, stay engaged with your my Social Security account. This portal allows you to:

- Monitor your payments
- Update your address or direct deposit information
- Get benefit verification letters
- Review your earnings record
- Track any changes to your benefits

Chapter Summary

Filing for Social Security represents a significant milestone in your retirement journey. While the process might seem daunting at first, proper preparation and understanding make it manageable. Remember that you don't have to navigate this alone – professional guidance can help ensure you make the most of your benefits.

In the next chapter, we'll explore advanced strategies for maximizing your Social Security benefits, including how to coordinate them with your other retirement income sources and special techniques for married couples.

NOTE:

Filing for Social Security benefits is a straightforward process that can be completed online, by phone, or in person at a Social Security office. Before applying, gather key documents such as your Social Security number, birth certificate, W-2 forms or self-employment tax returns, and banking information for direct deposit. It\u2019s best to file for benefits at least three months before you want payments to begin. For spousal or survivor benefits, additional documentation may be required, such as a marriage certificate or spouse\u2019s death certificate. Ensure all information is accurate to avoid delays, and consider consulting with a financial professional to confirm the timing aligns with your overall retirement plan.

Chapter 5: Strategies to Maximize Social Security

Robert and Patricia Anderson came to my office with a common dilemma. "We've saved carefully," Patricia explained, "but we're not sure how to turn our various retirement accounts into reliable monthly income." Robert nodded, adding, "And we want to make sure we're getting the most from Social Security." Their situation highlights a crucial truth: maximizing your Social Security benefits isn't just about when you claim – it's about how you coordinate these benefits with your overall retirement income strategy.

Creating Your Retirement Income Framework

Think of your retirement income like a three-legged stool. Social Security forms one leg, providing a guaranteed foundation. The second leg consists of any pensions or existing annuity income you may have. The third leg represents the income you'll need to generate from your savings and investments. The key to stability is ensuring all three legs work together effectively.

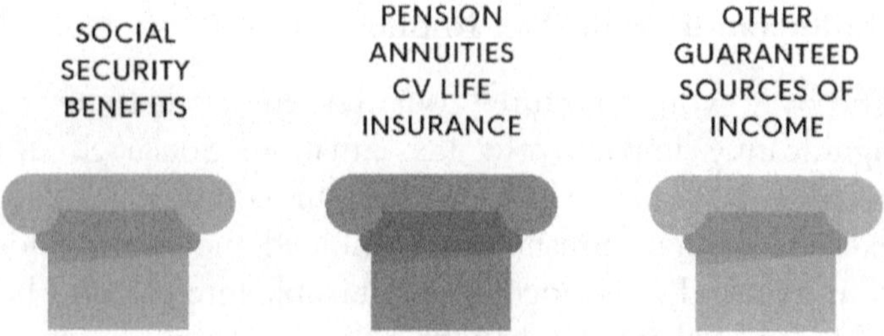

Coordinating Benefits with Other Income Sources

Creating a reliable monthly income in retirement requires careful orchestration of different income sources. Consider James and Marie, who recently retired. Their monthly expenses total $5,000, but their combined Social Security benefits only provide $3,200. James has a small pension of $800, leaving them with a $1,000 monthly income gap.

For James and Marie, like many retirees, this gap represents a significant challenge. They have savings in their 401(k)s and IRAs, but they worry about making this money last and protecting it from market downturns. This is where strategic use of a Fixed Indexed Annuity with a Guaranteed Income for Life rider can prove invaluable.

By converting a portion of their retirement savings into guaranteed lifetime income through a Fixed Indexed Annuity, they can fill their income gap while protecting their principal from market volatility. The optional inflation protection rider helps ensure their purchasing power remains stable over time, while the spousal continuation option provides security for the surviving spouse.

Understanding the Tax Implications

The way you structure your retirement income can significantly impact your tax situation. Social Security benefits become taxable when your combined income exceeds certain thresholds. Combined income includes your adjusted gross income, nontaxable interest, and half of your Social Security benefits.

Strategic withdrawal planning can help minimize the taxation of your benefits. For example, Carol, a recent retiree, learned she could reduce the taxation of her Social Security by carefully timing withdrawals from her various retirement accounts. By working with a financial professional, she developed a plan that balanced withdrawals between her tax-deferred accounts and her Roth IRA, helping keep more of her Social Security benefits tax-free.

Medicare Coordination Strategies

Healthcare costs represent a significant expense for most retirees, making Medicare coordination a crucial part of your Social Security strategy. The timing of your Medicare enrollment can affect both your coverage and your costs.

Most people become eligible for Medicare at age 65, but your specific situation might affect when you should enroll. If you're still working and covered by your employer's health plan, you might qualify for a Special Enrollment Period, allowing you to delay Medicare enrollment without penalty. However, this depends on factors like the size of your employer and whether you've started taking Social Security benefits.

Detailed Timeline for Coordinating Medicare and Social Security Benefits

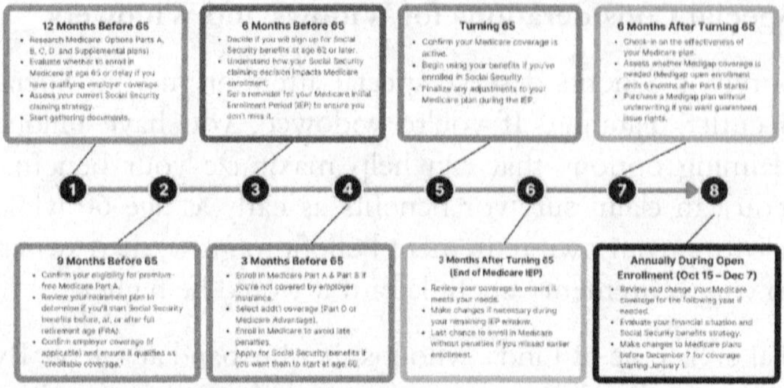

Maximizing Spousal Benefits

Married couples have unique opportunities to maximize their combined Social Security benefits through careful coordination. Consider Michael and Sarah, who have an age difference of five years. By carefully planning their claiming strategy, they can maximize their combined benefits and ensure the surviving spouse receives the highest possible survivor benefit.

For example, if Michael has earned significantly more than Sarah throughout their careers, it might make sense for him to delay claiming until age 70, maximizing his benefit. This strategy not only provides higher lifetime benefits for Michael but also ensures Sarah will receive a higher survivor benefit if he predeceases her.

Special Considerations for Widows and Widowers

Survivor benefits deserve special attention in your Social Security planning. If you're widowed, you have unique claiming options that can help maximize your benefits. You can claim survivor benefits as early as age 60 while allowing your own retirement benefit to grow, then switch to your retirement benefit later if it would be higher.

Take the case of Linda, who lost her husband at age 58. By understanding her options, she was able to claim survivor benefits at 60, allowing her own benefit to grow until age 70. This strategy provided immediate income while maximizing her long-term benefit amount.

Advanced Benefit Maximization Techniques

While some advanced claiming strategies have been eliminated by recent legislation, opportunities for maximizing benefits still exist. These often involve careful coordination of retirement timing, benefit claiming, and other income sources.

For instance, some retirees find that working part-time while delaying Social Security can provide multiple benefits. Not only does this approach allow their Social Security benefit to grow, but it can also help bridge the gap until larger benefits begin. Additionally, those extra years of earnings might replace lower-earning years in their benefit calculation, potentially increasing their monthly payment.

The Role of Fixed Indexed Annuities

When developing your Social Security maximization strategy, consider how a Fixed Indexed Annuity can complement your benefits. These products offer several advantages that align well with Social Security planning:

Guaranteed Lifetime Income: Like Social Security, a Fixed Indexed Annuity with a Guaranteed Income for Life rider provides income you can't outlive. This guaranteed income can help fill gaps in your monthly budget while providing peace of mind.

Protection from Market Risk: Your principal is protected from market downturns, helping ensure stable retirement income regardless of market conditions.

Inflation Protection Options: Optional riders can help your income keep pace with rising costs, similar to Social Security's cost-of-living adjustments.

Spousal Continuation: Many Fixed Indexed Annuities offer options to ensure income continues for a surviving spouse, complementing Social Security survivor benefits.

Creating Your Income Maximization Plan

Developing an effective Social Security maximization strategy requires careful consideration of your unique situation. Consider factors such as:

Your health and family history of longevity Your spouse's age and earnings record Your other sources of retirement income Your anticipated expenses in retirement Your tolerance for market risk Your tax situation

By taking all these factors into account, you can develop a comprehensive strategy that maximizes not just your Social Security benefits, but your overall retirement security.

Chapter Summary

Maximizing your Social Security benefits requires looking beyond just the timing of your claim. It involves coordinating your benefits with other income sources, understanding tax implications, and making informed decisions about Medicare enrollment. For many retirees, incorporating a Fixed Indexed Annuity into their strategy can help provide the guaranteed lifetime income needed to fill gaps and ensure financial security throughout retirement.

In our final chapter, we'll explore what the future holds for Social Security and how you can prepare for potential changes while maintaining confidence in your retirement plan.

NOTE:

To maximize your Social Security benefits, consider delaying your claim until after your full retirement age (FRA) to earn delayed retirement credits, increasing your benefit by up to 8% annually until age 70. If you are married, coordinate with your spouse to optimize benefits through strategies like claiming spousal benefits or delaying one spouse\u2019s benefits to maximize survivor benefits. Additionally, continue working if possible, to replace lower-earning years in your 35-year benefit calculation with higher-earning ones, which can increase your primary insurance amount (PIA). For those who started claiming early, a one-time do-over option, called a withdrawal of application, allows you to pause benefits and restart later for a higher amount. Consult a professional to tailor these strategies to your unique circumstances and retirement goals.

Chapter 6: The Future of Social Security

Mark and Jennifer, both in their mid-fifties, shared a common concern during our retirement planning session. "We keep hearing that Social Security is running out of money," Jennifer said. "Should we just claim early to make sure we get something?" This worry about Social Security's future is widespread, but making hasty decisions based on headlines can cost you thousands in lifetime benefits. Let's explore the real story behind Social Security's future and how you can prepare for what's ahead.

Understanding Social Security's Financial Structure

Social Security's financial structure is often misunderstood. Think of it as a pay-as-you-go system, where today's workers fund benefits for current retirees. This system has worked effectively for generations, but demographic changes are creating new challenges.

Social Security Trust Fund Projections

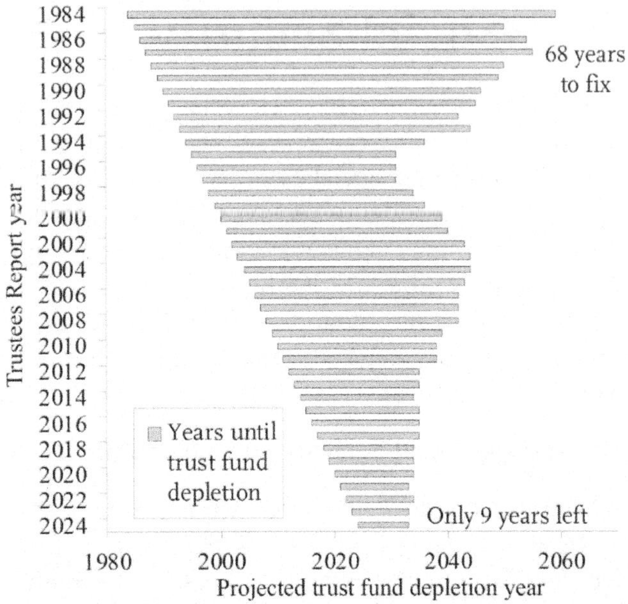

Source: 1984-2024 Social Security Trustees Reports.

The Real Story Behind the Headlines

When people say Social Security is "running out of money," they're referring to the depletion of the Trust Fund reserves, not the complete collapse of the system. Even if Congress makes no changes, Social Security would still collect enough in payroll taxes to pay about 80% of promised benefits after the trust fund's depletion.

Consider this analogy: If you had a monthly household budget of $5,000 but your income dropped to $4,000, you wouldn't be bankrupt – you'd need to make adjustments. Similarly, Social Security isn't facing bankruptcy but rather a need for adjustments to ensure full benefits can continue to be paid.

Historical Perspective on Social Security Changes

Social Security has evolved significantly since its creation in 1935. The program has weathered many challenges through careful adjustments and reforms. The 1983 amendments, for example, gradually raised the full retirement age and made other changes to strengthen the program's financial foundation.

Richard and Barbara, who retired in the early 1980s, remembered concerns similar to those we hear today. "People were worried the system wouldn't survive," Richard recalled. "But here we are, forty years later, and Social Security is still providing vital support to millions of retirees."

Potential Future Changes

While we can't predict exactly how Congress will address Social Security's funding challenges, we can look at commonly proposed solutions:

Adjusting the payroll tax cap: Currently, earnings above $168,600 (2024 figure) aren't subject to Social Security tax. Raising or eliminating this cap could significantly improve funding.

Gradual retirement age increases: Future retirees might see their full retirement age increase slightly, similar to previous adjustments.

Modified cost-of-living adjustments: Changes to how annual increases are calculated could help control long-term costs while maintaining purchasing power.

What This Means for Your Retirement Planning

Understanding potential changes helps inform your retirement strategy. Take the case of Emma, age 52, who's incorporating flexibility into her retirement plan. Rather than assuming Social Security will be her primary income source, she's working with a financial professional to create multiple income streams, including a Fixed Indexed Annuity with a Guaranteed Income for Life rider to provide reliable monthly income regardless of any changes to Social Security.

Creating a Resilient Retirement Plan

The key to confidence in your retirement future lies in building a plan that can weather various scenarios. This doesn't mean assuming the worst – it means being prepared for different possibilities while taking full advantage of current opportunities.

Building Retirement Income Security

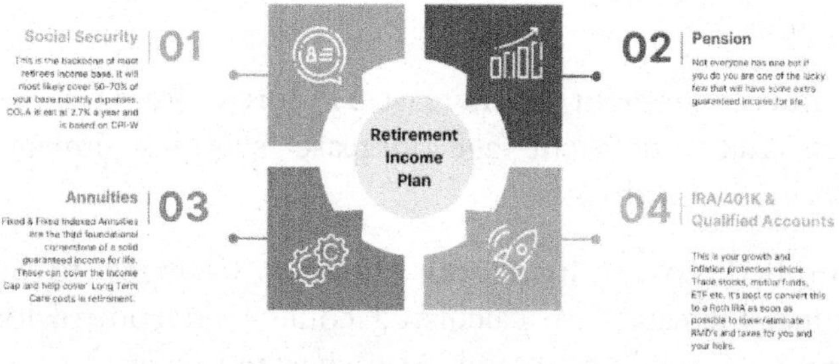

Consider how Thomas and Maria approached their retirement planning. Instead of letting concerns about Social Security's future drive them to claim early, they developed a comprehensive strategy. They calculated their essential expenses and created a foundation of guaranteed income through a combination of Social Security and a Fixed Indexed Annuity. This approach gave them confidence that their basic needs would be met, regardless of future changes to Social Security.

The Power of Guaranteed Income

In an uncertain future, guaranteed income becomes increasingly valuable. While Social Security provides one source of guaranteed lifetime income, many retirees find that adding other guaranteed income sources, such as Fixed Indexed Annuities with Guaranteed Income for Life riders, helps create a more secure retirement foundation.

These products offer several advantages that complement Social Security:

- Income you can't outlive
- Protection from market volatility
- Optional inflation protection
- Spousal continuation options

Taking Control of Your Retirement Future

Rather than worrying about factors outside your control, focus on elements you can influence. Start by understanding your current Social Security benefits and how they fit into your overall retirement picture. Calculate your essential expenses and identify any gaps between these expenses and your guaranteed income sources.

If you discover an income gap, consider how a Fixed Indexed Annuity might help provide the additional guaranteed income you need. These products can help ensure your essential expenses are covered, regardless of changes to Social Security or market conditions.

Planning for Multiple Scenarios

Smart retirement planning means being prepared for different possibilities. Work with a financial professional to develop strategies that can adapt to various scenarios. This might include:

Creating multiple income streams to reduce reliance on any single source Building flexibility into your retirement timing Maintaining emergency savings for unexpected expenses Regular review and adjustment of your plan as circumstances change

The Role of Professional Guidance

Navigating retirement planning in an uncertain environment requires informed decision-making. A financial professional can help you:

Understand how potential Social Security changes might affect your specific situation Identify strategies to maximize your benefits under current rules Create a comprehensive retirement income plan Select appropriate products to fill any income gaps

The Importance of Starting Now

While the future of Social Security may include changes, the worst approach is to let uncertainty paralyze your retirement planning. The sooner you begin preparing, the more options you'll have to create a secure retirement income strategy.

Chapter Summary

While Social Security faces funding challenges, the system will continue to provide vital support for retirees. Rather than making fear-based decisions, focus on creating a comprehensive retirement plan that includes multiple sources of guaranteed income. By understanding potential changes and preparing accordingly, you can build confidence in your retirement future regardless of how Social Security evolves.

Looking Ahead

Remember that you don't have to navigate these challenges alone. Professional guidance can help you create a retirement income strategy that maximizes your Social Security benefits while ensuring your essential expenses are covered through guaranteed income sources like Fixed Indexed Annuities. Take the first step today by scheduling a retirement income planning session to review your specific situation and explore your options for creating a secure retirement future.

NOTE:

The future of Social Security faces challenges due to an aging population, longer life expectancies, and declining worker-to-beneficiary ratios. Current projections from the Social Security Trustees indicate that the trust fund reserves may be depleted by 2034, at which point benefits could be reduced to approximately 78% of promised levels if no changes are made. However, potential solutions, such as increasing payroll taxes, raising the full retirement age, or adjusting benefit formulas, could address the funding shortfall. While Social Security is unlikely to disappear, future retirees should plan for potential changes by diversifying their income sources and considering strategies to reduce reliance on Social Security benefits. Staying informed about legislative updates and adjusting your retirement plan accordingly is essential.

Conclusion: Taking Control of Your Social Security Future

Throughout this book, we've explored the many facets of Social Security and how it fits into your retirement picture. Like Sarah, whom we met in Chapter 1, you might have started this journey feeling overwhelmed by the complexity of Social Security decisions. Now, armed with knowledge and understanding, you can approach these decisions with confidence.

Your Social Security Journey

Think of your Social Security claiming decision as one piece of a larger retirement puzzle. While the decision about when to claim benefits is important, it's equally crucial to understand how these benefits work together with your other retirement income sources. Remember James and Marie from Chapter 5, who discovered that coordinating their Social Security benefits with a Fixed Indexed Annuity helped them create the secure retirement income they desired.

The Power of Informed Decisions

Throughout this book, we've seen how small decisions can have significant long-term impacts on your retirement security. Consider the example of Linda, who increased her lifetime benefits by over $100,000 simply by understanding her survivor benefit options. Or Michael and Sarah, who maximized their combined benefits through careful coordination of their claiming strategies.

Your Social Security decisions deserve careful consideration because they affect not just your immediate future, but potentially decades of retirement. The difference between an optimal and suboptimal claiming strategy could mean tens or even hundreds of thousands of dollars over your lifetime. More importantly, it could mean the difference between financial stress and financial security in your later years.

Beyond Social Security

While Social Security provides an important foundation, we've learned that most retirees need additional sources of guaranteed income to maintain their desired lifestyle. The monthly income gap between Social Security benefits and essential expenses represents a critical planning challenge. However, solutions exist to bridge this gap effectively.

Fixed Indexed Annuities with Guaranteed Income for Life riders have emerged as powerful tools for creating reliable retirement income. These products offer features that complement Social Security beautifully: guaranteed lifetime income, protection from market volatility, optional inflation protection, and spousal continuation options. Together with Social Security, they can create a strong foundation of guaranteed income to cover your essential expenses.

The Path Forward

As you move forward with your Social Security planning, remember that you don't have to make these decisions alone. Professional guidance can help you navigate the complexities and create a comprehensive retirement income strategy that maximizes your benefits while ensuring your essential expenses are covered.

Consider scheduling a retirement income planning session to:

- Review your Social Security claiming options
- Calculate your expected benefits
- Identify any income gaps
- Explore solutions for creating guaranteed lifetime income
- Develop a comprehensive retirement income strategy

Final Thoughts

Social Security represents one of America's most successful social programs, providing retirement security for millions of people. While the system may face challenges in the future, it will continue to play a vital role in retirement planning. By understanding your benefits and making informed decisions about when and how to claim them, you can make the most of this important retirement resource.

Remember that retirement planning isn't just about maximizing numbers on a page – it's about creating the security and confidence you need to enjoy your retirement years. Whether your retirement dreams include traveling, spending time with family, pursuing hobbies, or simply relaxing, a solid foundation of guaranteed income can help make those dreams possible.

Your Next Steps

As you finish this book, take a moment to consider your next steps. Review the worksheets in the appendix, gather your Social Security statements, and start thinking about your retirement income needs. Most importantly, don't let uncertainty about the future prevent you from taking action today.

The path to retirement security begins with a single step. Whether you're years away from retirement or already contemplating when to claim your benefits, the time to start planning is now. Reach out to a financial professional who can help you create a comprehensive retirement income strategy that maximizes your Social Security benefits while ensuring your retirement dreams become reality.

Remember, your retirement journey is unique to you. The strategies and approaches we've discussed can be customized to fit your specific situation, goals, and needs. By taking action now and seeking professional guidance, you can move forward with confidence, knowing you're making informed decisions about your retirement future.

Thank you for allowing me to guide you through the complexities of Social Security. May your retirement years be filled with security, joy, and the freedom to pursue your dreams.

NOTE:

Planning for Social Security is a critical component of a comprehensive retirement strategy. By understanding how benefits are calculated, the timing of your claim, and potential tax implications, you can make informed decisions that maximize your income and minimize financial risks. Remember, Social Security is just one piece of your retirement puzzle. Pairing it with other strategies, such as Roth conversions, tax-loss harvesting, and diversified investment planning, can create a robust and resilient financial future. Stay informed about legislative changes, consult trusted professionals, and revisit your plan regularly to adapt to life\u2019s changes and ensure your retirement goals are met.

Appendices: Tools and Resources

Appendix A: Retirement Income Planning Worksheet

This comprehensive worksheet will help you calculate your retirement income needs and identify potential gaps in your retirement income plan.

Monthly Expense Calculator

Essential Living Expenses:

Copy

Category Current Retirement

Housing

Mortgage/Rent $_______ $_______

Property Tax $_______ $_______

Insurance $_______ $_______

Utilities $_______ $_______

Maintenance $_______ $_______

Healthcare

Medicare Premiums $_______ $_______

Supplemental Ins. $_______ $_______

Out of Pocket $_______ $_______

Basic Living

Food/Groceries $_______ $_______

Transportation $_______ $_______

Phone/Internet $_______ $_______

Basic Clothing $_______ $_______

Total Essential $_______ $_______

Guaranteed Income Sources

Copy

Source Monthly Amount

Social Security (Self) $_______

Social Security (Spouse)$_______

Pension $_______

Existing Annuities $_______

Other Guaranteed $_______

Total Guaranteed $_______

Calculate Your Income Gap

Copy

Total Essential Expenses $_______

- Total Guaranteed Income $_______

= Monthly Income Gap $_______

Appendix B: Social Security Benefits Estimator

Use this worksheet to estimate your Social Security benefits at different claiming ages.

Go to https://www.ssa.gov/ and get your Social Security benefit amount at ages 62 thru 70.

Your Full Retirement Age (FRA) Benefit: $_______

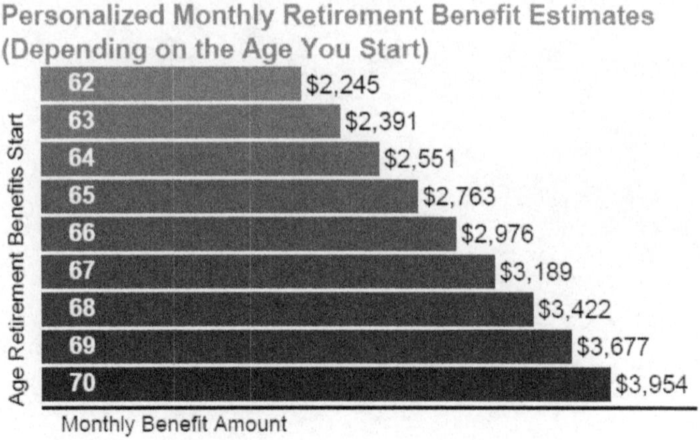

Claiming Age	Percentage of FRA	Monthly Benefit
62	70-75%	$_______
63	75-80%	$_______
64	80-85%	$_______
65	85-90%	$_______

66	90-95%	$_______
67	100%	$_______
68	108%	$_______
69	116%	$_______
70	124%	$_______

Appendix C: Medicare Decision Guide

Medicare Initial Enrollment Period Timeline

https://www.medicare.gov/

If you sign up:	Coverage starts:
Before the month you turn 65	The month you turn 65
The month you turn 65, or during the 3 months after	The next month

Medicare Coverage Options Worksheet

Part A (Hospital) ☐ Yes ☐ No

Part B (Medical) ☐ Yes ☐ No

Part C (Medicare Advantage) ☐ Yes ☐ No

Part D (Prescription) ☐ Yes ☐ No

Medigap Policy ☐ Yes ☐ No

Appendix D: Social Security Filing Checklist

Required Documents

- Birth Certificate
- Social Security Card
- Marriage Certificate (if applicable)
- Divorce Decree (if applicable)
- Death Certificate (for survivor benefits)
- Military Service Papers
- W-2 Forms or Tax Returns
- Bank Account Information

Filing Timeline

3 Months Before Desired Start Date:

- Gather required documents
- Review benefit options
- Create my Social Security account

2 Months Before:

- Calculate optimal claiming age

- Consider Medicare coordination
- Review income tax implications

1 Month Before:

- Submit application
- Set up direct deposit
- Plan for income gap period

Appendix E: Fixed Indexed Annuity Evaluation Guide

When considering a Fixed Indexed Annuity to fill your income gap, evaluate these key features:

Income Rider Analysis

Feature	Notes
Guaranteed Income Rate	_______
Income Start Date Options	_______
Spousal Continuation	_______
Inflation Protection	_______
Flexibility Options	_______

Questions to Ask

1. What is the guaranteed minimum income?
2. How does the income increase over time?
3. What happens to the benefit if I need to access principal?
4. How does the spousal benefit work?
5. What are the fees associated with the riders?

Resource Directory

Social Security Administration

- Website: www.ssa.gov

- Toll-Free: 1-800-772-1213
- TTY: 1-800-325-0778

Medicare Resources

- Website: www.medicare.gov
- Toll-Free: 1-800-MEDICARE
- State Health Insurance Assistance Program (SHIP)

Retirement Planning Resources

For a complimentary retirement income planning session, contact:

Boom Retirement Solutions

Our retirement income specialists can help you:

- Analyze your Social Security claiming options
- Calculate your retirement income gap
- Explore guaranteed income solutions
- Create a comprehensive retirement income plan

Glossary of Terms

AIME (Average Indexed Monthly Earnings) : The average of your 35 highest-earning years, adjusted for inflation, used to calculate your Social Security benefit.

Cost of Living Adjustment (COLA) : Annual increases in Social Security benefits based on inflation.

Fixed Indexed Annuity : An insurance product that provides guaranteed income while protecting principal from market losses.

Full Retirement Age (FRA) : The age at which you're eligible for 100% of your Social Security benefit.

Primary Insurance Amount (PIA) : Your basic Social Security benefit at full retirement age.

Survivor Benefits : Benefits paid to eligible family members after a worker's death.

These appendices are designed to be practical tools to help you implement the strategies discussed in this book. Use them as working documents, filling in the information relevant to your situation and updating them as your circumstances change.

Index

For Additional Support:

We are here to help. Request your free Social Security Analysis and retirement Income Plan. If you would like personalized guidance in maximizing your Social Security benefits and creating a comprehensive retirement income strategy, please contact:

Boom Retirement Solutions

(888) 839-1611

SCAN TO SCHEDULE

FLOWCODE

PRIVACY.FLOWCODE.COM

AN APPOINTMENT

For a free copy of our other book "12 Smart Tax Strategies for Retirees" send an email to jeff@boomretirement.com and in the Subject Line write "Free Book 12 Smart Tax Strategies"

Made in the USA
Monee, IL
04 November 2026

67381907R00056

The United States Army War College

The United States Army War College educates and develops leaders for service at the strategic level while advancing knowledge in the global application of Landpower.

The purpose of the United States Army War College is to produce graduates who are skilled critical thinkers and complex problem solvers. Concurrently, it is our duty to the U.S. Army to also act as a "think factory" for commanders and civilian leaders at the strategic level worldwide and routinely engage in discourse and debate concerning the role of ground forces in achieving national security objectives.

SSI
STRATEGIC STUDIES INSTITUTE

The Strategic Studies Institute publishes national security and strategic research and analysis to influence policy debate and bridge the gap between military and academia.

CENTER for STRATEGIC LEADERSHIP and DEVELOPMENT CSLD
U.S. ARMY WAR COLLEGE

The Center for Strategic Leadership and Development contributes to the education of world class senior leaders, develops expert knowledge, and provides solutions to strategic Army issues affecting the national security community.

PKSOI

The Peacekeeping and Stability Operations Institute provides subject matter expertise, technical review, and writing expertise to agencies that develop stability operations concepts and doctrines.

U.S. Army War College
SLDR
Senior Leader Development and Resiliency

The Senior Leader Development and Resiliency program supports the United States Army War College's lines of effort to educate strategic leaders and provide well-being education and support by developing self-awareness through leader feedback and leader resiliency.

SCHOOL OF STRATEGIC LANDPOWER
U. S. Army War College

The School of Strategic Landpower develops strategic leaders by providing a strong foundation of wisdom grounded in mastery of the profession of arms, and by serving as a crucible for educating future leaders in the analysis, evaluation, and refinement of professional expertise in war, strategy, operations, national security, resource management, and responsible command.

The U.S. Army Heritage and Education Center acquires, conserves, and exhibits historical materials for use to support the U.S. Army, educate an international audience, and honor Soldiers—past and present.

STRATEGIC STUDIES INSTITUTE

The Strategic Studies Institute (SSI) is part of the U.S. Army War College and is the strategic-level study agent for issues related to national security and military strategy with emphasis on geostrategic analysis.

The mission of SSI is to use independent analysis to conduct strategic studies that develop policy recommendations on:

- Strategy, planning, and policy for joint and combined employment of military forces;
- Regional strategic appraisals;
- The nature of land warfare;
- Matters affecting the Army's future;
- The concepts, philosophy, and theory of strategy; and,
- Other issues of importance to the leadership of the Army.

Studies produced by civilian and military analysts concern topics having strategic implications for the Army, the Department of Defense, and the larger national security community.

In addition to its studies, SSI publishes special reports on topics of special or immediate interest. These include edited proceedings of conferences and topically oriented roundtables, expanded trip reports, and quick-reaction responses to senior Army leaders.

The Institute provides a valuable analytical capability within the Army to address strategic and other issues in support of Army participation in national security policy formulation.